this gift is for

_____

from

_____

MOMENTS OF BLESSING

Gary Smalley
and
John Trent, Ph.D.

A
JANET
THOMA
BOOK

THOMAS NELSON PUBLISHERS
NASHVILLE

*All of us long to be
accepted by others.*

The search for parental blessing is actually centuries old. For sons and daughters in biblical times, receiving their father's blessing was a momentous event.

A blessing in Old Testament
times gave children a sense of
being highly valued by their
parents and even pictured a
special future for them.

At a specific point in their lives, when given the blessing, children would hear words of encouragement, love, and acceptance from their parents.

In Bible times this blessing was primarily reserved for one special occasion. In contrast, parents today can decide to build elements of blessing into their children's lives daily.

*the first element
of the blessing:
meaningful touch*

In the Scriptures, touch played
an important part in the
bestowal of the family blessing.

Symbolically, touch was a
graphic picture of transferring
power or blessing from one
person to another.

Your spouse and others need meaningful touch. However, children are particularly affected by touch deprivation.

Sometimes the absence of touch can so affect a child that he or she spends a lifetime reaching out for arms that will never embrace him or her.

Touching a child on the
shoulder, holding hands with
your spouse, stopping to ruffle
someone's hair—all these acts
can change how you are
viewed by others.

There are two important
reasons why meaningful touch
is so special. First, there is a
symbolic meaning attached to
touching, and second, there
are tremendous physical
benefits to touching.

In the Old Testament, touch was a symbolic, yet graphic, picture of transferring power or blessing from one person to another.

Even today, the symbolic
meaning of touch is powerful.

One researcher has made numerous studies on the effects of the physical benefits of touching. She found that both the toucher and the one being touched receive a physiological benefit.

Hugs and kisses were also a
part of meaningful touch
pictured in the Scriptures.

Residents of a nursing home and a local animal shelter were brought together. Those residents who had a pet to touch and hold not only lived longer than those without, but they also had a more positive attitude about life.

In a UCLA study, it was found
that to maintain emotional
and physical health, men and
women need eight to ten
meaningful touches each day!

So healthy is meaningful touch, we ought to listen to the words of Ralph Waldo Emerson: ''I never like the giving of the hand, unless the entire body accompanies it!''

Jesus was a model of someone who communicated the blessing—"And He took them up in His arms, put His hands on them, and blessed them" (Mark 10:13-16).

If we want to be people who give the blessing to others, we will include meaningful touch in our contacts with loved ones.

*the second element of
the blessing: spoken
words*

The second element of the blessing is a spoken message. In many homes today, words of love and acceptance are seldom heard.

A tragic misconception parents sometimes share is that simply being present communicates the blessing . . . . A blessing becomes so only when it is spoken.

For a child in search of the blessing, the major thing silence communicates is confusion.

A lack of negative words does
not translate into a spoken
blessing.

Many people can clearly
remember words of praise their
parents spoke years ago.
Others can remember, still
more clearly, negative words
they heard.

If you are a parent, your children desperately need to hear a spoken blessing from you. If you are married, your wife or husband needs to hear words of love and acceptance on a regular basis.

In the very beginning, God "spoke" and the world came into being (Gen. 1:3).

When God sent us His Son to communicate His love and complete His plan of salvation, it was His Word which "became flesh and dwelt among us" (John 1:14).

God has always been a God who communicates His blessing through spoken words.

Both people and relationships
suffer in the absence of spoken
words of love, encouragement,
and support-words of blessing.

When a spoken blessing is withheld in a marriage, unmet needs for security and acceptance act like sulfuric acid and eat away at a relationship.

By deciding to communicate
words of love and acceptance
verbally, we do not have to
send away a child, spouse, or
friend in need.

Without words of love,
acceptance, and
encouragement, children often
grow up traveling roads that
lead to unhealthy extremes.

Are words or their absence really that powerful? Solomon thought so. He shocks us into reality with his words, "Death and life are in the power of the tongue."

If the truth be known, the
reason many people hesitate
to bless their children or others
with spoken words of love and
acceptance is that their parents
never gave them this part of
the blessing.

We put spoken words of blessing into practice in our homes and relationships by deciding to speak up rather than clam up.

Don't delay. Time passes so quickly. Please don't let an important person leave your life without hearing the second element of the blessing—spoken words.

the third element of the blessing: expressing high value

To value something means to attach honor to it.

Words of blessing should carry with them the recognition that this person is valuable and has redeeming qualities. In the Scriptures, recognition is based on who they are, not simply on their performance.

Every person today needs the blessing to feel truly loved and secure about himself or herself. This concept of valuing another person is so important that we believe it can be found at the heart of every healthy relationship.

Telling children they are
valuable can be difficult for
many parents.

Children may hear an
occasional word of praise, but
only if they perform well on a
task. When words of value are
only linked to a child's
performance, they lose much
of their value.

Children who have to perform to get a blessing retain a nagging uncertainty about whether they ever really received it.

We need to find a better way
to communicate a message of
high value and acceptance.

The key to communicating high value is in using word pictures.

Word pictures can be used in
any relationship to
communicate words of high
value.

In choosing a word picture to communicate high value, try to capture a trait or physical attribute of the person in an everyday object. Match the emotional meaning behind the trait you want to praise.

Word pictures, used over time,
capture our attention in spite
of our defenses, and get across
a message of high value.

Jesus illustrated the undeveloped traits of a person by changing Simon's name to Peter ("rock" in Greek). Peter initially didn't act like a rock of strength, but after the resurrection Peter became the rock he was pictured to be.

A well-known saying tells us that one picture is worth a thousand words. When we link a word picture with a message of high value, we multiply our message a thousand times.

the fourth element of the blessing: picturing a special future

When it comes to predictions about their future, children are literalists. For this reason, communicating a special future to a child is an important part of parents giving the blessing.

When a person feels in his or her heart that the future is hopeful and something to look forward to, it can greatly affect his or her attitude on life.

If children hear only words
that predict relationship
problems or personal
inadequacies, they can turn
and travel down a hurtful path
that has been pictured for
them.

Words that picture a special future act like a campfire on a dark night. They can draw a person toward the warmth of genuine concern and fulfilled potential.

Picturing a special future for a child, spouse, or friend can help bring out the best in his or her life. It gives them a positive direction to strive toward and surrounds them with hope.

Jeremiah assures us of the special future we have in our relationship with the Lord: "For I know the thoughts that I think toward you, says the Lord, thoughts of peace and not of evil, to give you a future and a hope" (Jer. 29:11).

Time and time again, God
gives us a picture of our special
future with Him in His word.

If a parent pictures for a child that his or her value in life is low, that child will find it difficult to rise above these words.

Those who desire to give their children the blessing will provide the room for these boys and girls to grow by encouraging their potential and by picturing a special future for them.

Are you providing your children, spouse, or intimate friends with a blessing that pictures a special future for them? Wherever the blessing is given or received, words that picture a special future are always spoken.

the fifth element of the blessing: an active commitment

Words alone cannot
communicate the blessing;
they need to be backed with a
commitment to do everything
possible to help the one
blessed to be successful.

As a child in school, a teacher who is willing to make an active commitment to your learning can make your educational experience a success.

In the school of life, children
desperately need parents who
will make an active
commitment to them.

In areas in which the children are weak, they need to be encouraged and built up. They need to be hugged and verbally praised for their strengths.

The mortar that holds the first
four elements of the blessing
together is an active
commitment—the fifth element
of the blessing.

Words of blessing alone are
not enough. They need to be
backed by the commitment of
a person to see the blessing
come to pass.

We need to take action if we are to give the blessing.

The first step in expressing an active commitment to your loved one is to commit the person being blessed to the Lord.

Wise parents will model the
practice of pastors every
Sunday by saying, "May the
Lord bless you." In so doing
they are recognizing that any
strength they have comes from
God.

Even the breath of life we
have to speak words of
blessing comes from God.

Another important reason to commit our children to the Lord when we bless them is that this teaches them that God is personally concerned with their life and welfare.

The second step in expressing
an active commitment to our
loved ones is to commit our
lives to their best interests.

Blessing our children involves understanding their unique bent. In addition, it means being willing to do what is best for that person—even if it means having to correct them when they are wrong.

It should not surprise us that
blessing and discipline go
hand in hand.

If we genuinely love someone,
we will not allow him or her
to stray into sin or be hurt in
some way without trying to
correct our loved one.

A way we can demonstrate
an active commitment to our
children is to become a
student of those we wish
to bless.

If we have struggled in our relationships with our loved ones or if we haven't been close to them in the past, we must be lovingly persistent in encouraging them to talk.

A practical way to get started
in becoming a student of
those we wish to bless is to
listen to them with our full
attention.

Active listening is an important
part of communicating
acceptance and blessing to our
loved ones.

Commitment is costly. You
must commit time, energy, and
effort to see the blessing
become a reality in
someone's life.

Giving our children the
blessing is like casting bread
upon the waters. In years to
come, they too will rise up
and bless us.

Our prayer for every person who reads this book is that you will become a person of blessing. The cost is genuine commitment, but the rewards can last a lifetime and beyond.

**Library of Congress
Cataloging-in-Publication Data**

Smalley, Gary
  Moments of blessing / by Gary Smalley,
John Trent.
    p.   cm.
  ISBN 0-8407-7810-4
  1. Family—Religious life.   2. Parenting—
Religious aspects—Christianity.   3. Blessing and
cursing.   4. Self-esteem—Religious aspects—
Christianity.   I. Trent, John T.   II. Title.
BV4526.2.S5266   1993
249—dc20   92-37891
                                              CIP

Printed in Singapore.
1 2 3 4 — 95 94 93 92